Ready, Get Set, Whoa!

By The Radlauers
Ed, Robin, Ruth, and Dan

AN ELK GROVE BOOK
CHILDRENS PRESS, CHICAGO

Cover photo by Dan Radlauer

Library of Congress Cataloging in Publication Data

Main entry under title:
Ready, get set, whoa!

SUMMARY: Photographs and simple text illustrate the basic techniques of horseback riding.
"An Elk Grove book."
1. Horesemanship—Juvenile literature. [1. Horsemanship] I. Radlauer, Edward.
SF309.2.R4 798'.2 74-8566
ISBN 0-516-07420-2

Printed in the United States of America.

1 2 3 4 5 6 7 8 9 10 11 12 13 14 15 R 80 79 78 77 76 75 74

Ready, Get Set, Go Books

Ready

Motorcycle Mania
Flying Mania

Get Set

Fast, Faster, Fastest
Wild Wheels

GO

Soap Box Racing
Ready, Get Set, Whoa!

Ready, get set, whoa.
Whoa is right!
Before you ride a horse,
there are some things you need to learn
and some things you need to do.

Whoa is right!

Before you ride a horse, you need to learn how to ride. When you learn to ride, you will find out how to sit and how to hold the reins.

Then you can learn how to cue, or tell, the horse what to do. You cue, or tell, a horse to walk, jog, or lope. A jog is a slow trot, and a lope is a slow gallop. The cue to stop is WHOA.

You can cue a horse to do almost anything. But a horse should walk or jog, lope or gallop only when you give the right cue.

You can cue a horse to do almost anything.

If you ride a horse western style, you ride in a western style saddle. Your horse wears a western style bridle, and you wear western clothes.

When you ride, you sit tall and straight, straight but not stiff. Put your feet in the stirrups, but not too far into the stirrups.

You hold both reins with your left hand. Your right hand holds the ends of the reins down at your right side.

A good rider can show you how.

When you want to cue a horse to go, you squeeze with your legs and say, "Walk." If the horse doesn't go, squeeze again and say, "Walk!" You must sound like you mean it. If the horse doesn't go with a squeeze, you may have to kick a little with your heels.

To get a horse to stop, say, "Whoa," and pull back on the reins. Pull back on the reins gently. If the horse does what you say, pat his neck gently. A pat on the neck shows the horse that you like what he did.

When you can make a horse walk and stop, you can learn to jog, then to lope. It's best to have a good rider show you how.

A pat on the neck shows the horse you like what he did.

Horse riding is safe when a rider knows all about horses. A good rider knows which end is which and all the parts of the horse.

It's easy to find the head and the neck, the mane and the tail, and all four legs. But which is the barrel, and where are the withers? Where is the pole, and which is the gaskin? Everyone knows where to find the eyes and the ears, but now you can see which is the cannon bone, and where the hocks and the stifle joint are.

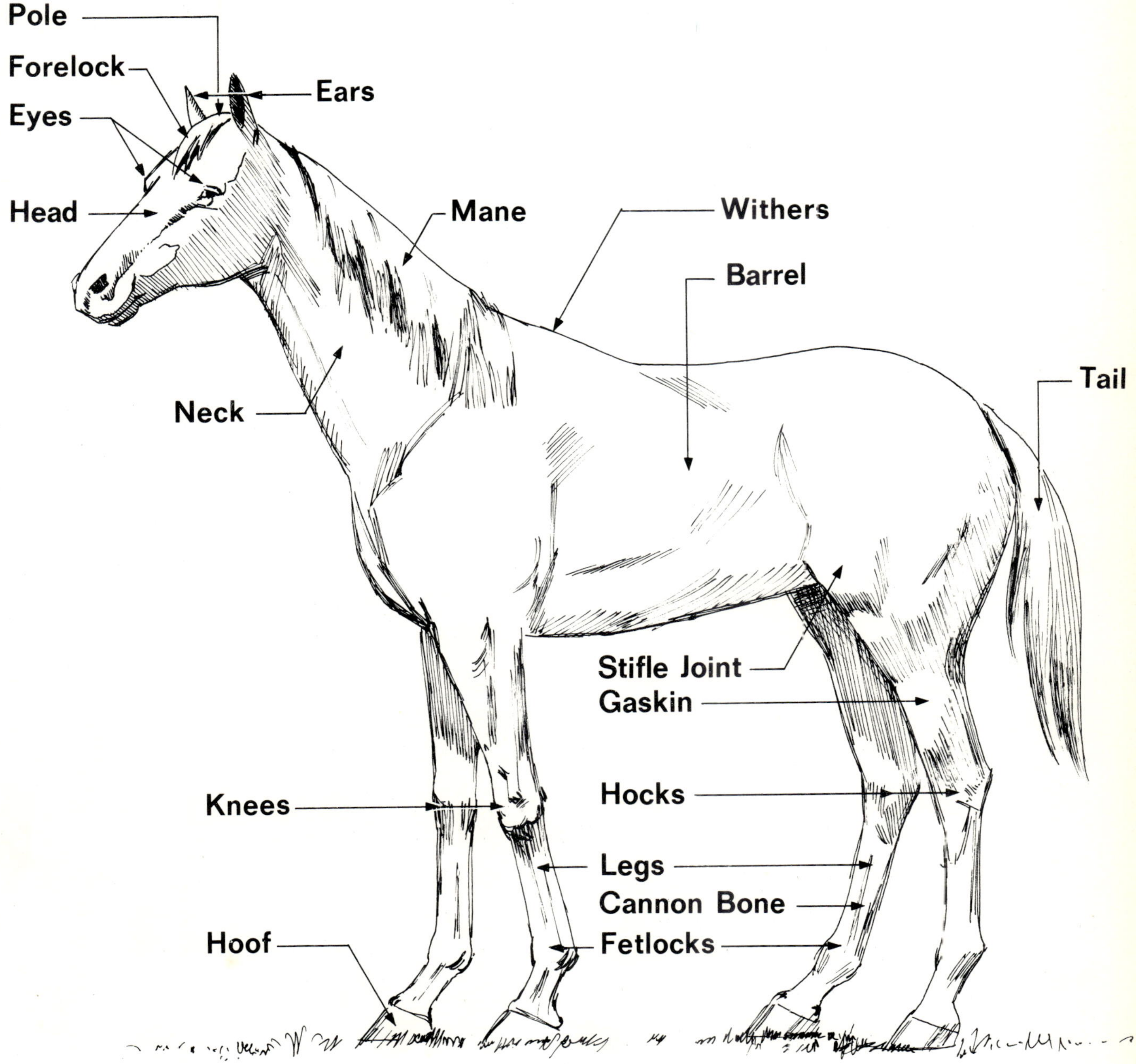
Pole
Forelock
Eyes
Head
Ears
Mane
Withers
Barrel
Tail
Neck
Stifle Joint
Gaskin
Knees
Hocks
Legs
Cannon Bone
Hoof
Fetlocks

A horse has two eyes, but they are not like your eyes. He can look at things in front of him, and he can see things beside him. But a horse doesn't always understand what he sees.

He may think a pile of junk means danger, and danger makes a horse spook. When a horse spooks, he may jump or turn and run away as fast as he can. But if you talk to him and let him look, he will understand what he sees.

Sometimes a horse sleeps standing up, with his eyes open. If you surprise a sleeping horse, he may spook. That's why you should always talk as you come near one.

Horses are safe to be near when you understand what they might do.

Let your horse look at things that might spook him.

Some people like English style riding. When English style riders do jumping, they wear hard hats. A jumper uses an English style saddle called a hunt seat. The hunt seat is good for jumping.

Other English riders use a different saddle, a park seat, and wear a different style of clothes. The horse wears a different kind of bridle, and the rider holds the reins with both hands.

Hunt seat, or park seat, English horses have four legs and eat hay, just the same as western horses do.

Hunt seat.

Park seat.

When you choose a horse, you should think about two things. Does it have a good disposition, a good way of acting? And is it healthy?

A good disposition means you can put a halter or bridle on the horse without any trouble. A horse with a good disposition works with you and doesn't give you a lot of trouble.

A healthy horse has a clean shiny coat. Its legs are straight without any bumps on the straight bones. Its eyes look bright and shiny, and the body is round but not fat.

A horse with a good disposition is easy to halter or bridle.

There are many breeds of horses. A breed that western riders like is called the quarter horse.

It's a whole horse, but it's called a quarter horse because cowboys like to use it for a quarter-mile race.

A quarter horse is also good for ranch work, trail riding, and showing.

Quarter horse. A good breed for western riders.

Some English riders like thoroughbreds. Thoroughbreds make good jumpers. Many English riders like Arab horses, and some like to ride in Arab costumes. Do you think the horse likes his Arab costume?

This Arab horse and rider have Arab costumes.

Small riders like small horses. Some Arab horses are small, but ponies are smaller. A hackney pony is small. A Welsh pony is smaller than a hackney, and the Shetland pony is smaller than a Welsh. The Shetland pony is the smallest breed of pony or horse.

A hackney pony pulls a hackney cart.

A hackney pony pulls a hackney cart.

To have a horse of your own, you need a corral or pasture with room for the horse to move around. In a corral or pasture your horse needs a trough for feed and a trough for water.

You need tools to keep a corral clean, and tools to keep the horse clean

Having a horse means lots of work. You feed your horse every morning and every night—whether you ride or not. You have to clean the corral almost every day—whether you want to or not.

How much feed and water does a horse need? Most horses eat a bale of hay every week. The water trough should be very big and be filled two or three times a day.

You need tools to keep corral and horse clean.

To have a horse that's healthy and fun to ride, you should ride every day. Before you ride, you groom your horse.

Think of safety as you groom. Keep an eye on the horse's feet so he won't step on you. When you think of safety, you won't get hurt.

Move smoothly when you groom. If you are jumpy, your horse will be jumpy, too. Moving smoothly, you brush and brush, then brush some more. Then you comb and comb and comb some more.

When the combing and brushing are done, it's time to clean the hoofs. You use a hoof pick and make sure that no rocks or sticks are in the hoof. A clean hoof won't pick up rocks or sticks while you ride.

You comb the mane and comb the tail.

After the horse is groomed, the saddle goes on over a saddle pad. Putting the saddle on isn't as easy as it looks in a cowboy movie. A western saddle is heavy, but you can make it easy to lift. With the left side of the saddle against you, fold the right stirrup and the cinch across the seat. Then lift the saddle gently onto the horse's back.

Pull the cinch up under the horse's belly and tighten it. Take care not to pinch the horse as you tighten the cinch. No horse likes a pinch from a cinch. Would you?

Every time you get on a horse, check to see if you need to tighten the cinch. With a cinch that's not tight, you and your saddle could end up under the horse's belly. That's not such a good way to ride.

Lifting a western saddle isn't easy, but it helps to know how.

Now it's time to put the bridle on. A good horse will take the bit of the bridle into his mouth with no trouble.

With your right hand between his ears, hold the top of the bridle. Take the bit in your left hand and put it gently against the horse's teeth. He should take the bit into his mouth. If you have trouble, put your thumb into the side of his mouth where there are no teeth. The taste of your thumb makes a horse open his mouth to take the bit.

If you still have trouble, put some jelly on the bit. The taste of jelly makes your horse like the bit.

When the bridle is on, the reins go over the neck, and you're ready to get on. Stand on the left side of the horse. Check the cinch to be sure it's tight. Then put your left foot into the stirrup and pull yourself up. Put your right foot in the right stirrup and sit in the saddle.

A good horse will take the bit without any trouble.

OK. Now you're ready.
It's not, "Ready, get set, whoa!"
It's time to get ready, get set, and
GO!

Ready, get set, go!

The Beginning?